the TULA PINK
COLORING BOOK

75+ SIGNATURE DESIGNS
IN FANCIFUL COLORING PAGES

Fons&Porter

CINCINNATI, OHIO

INTRODUCTION

I am a doodler by nature, an illustrator by training and a fabric designer by profession. As a fabric designer, my main focus is creating drawings that repeat in every direction, fitting together like perfect interlocking puzzle pieces. Color has always been the enduring thread that has tied all of my artistic interests together. Color sets the mood and determines the personality of the drawing.

My lifelong love affair with color began with coloring books. A pristine white page filled with crisp black lines and a brand new box of crayons can be a magical thing. A coloring book is an open-ended question; the framework has been established but the direction that it takes is up to the crayons. A green frog is simply a frog but a purple frog can be something else entirely.

It makes sense that years of sharpening my craft as an illustrator should bring me back here, to a coloring book. In these pages you will find a menagerie of creatures and forms, from frogs and owls to bugs, fish, flowers and geometry. Nature presents the most incredible study of shapes. Using wildlife as a foundation, I can create an image that is instantly familiar while stretching the boundaries of the subject's composition. A frenzy of paislies, swirls and stripes can create the silhouette of an owl. Leaves and dots can come together to form a rabbit crouching in a field of wildflowers. The possibilities are endless, and it's that idea of reinvention that consumes me and makes up the bulk of my work.

The drawings collected here represent a history of my fabric designs, extracted from their infinite repeating loop and reduced to their most essential lines and shapes. All they are waiting for is a little bit of free-spirited coloring. I have posed the question—how will you answer?

ACACIA
Arrowheads

ACACIA
Quills

ACACIA
Hummingbird

ACACIA
Pineapple Slices

ACACIA

Raccoon

THE BIRDS AND THE BEES
Bees Knees

THE BIRDS AND THE BEES
Little Bits

THE BIRDS AND THE BEES

Lazy Stripe

THE BIRDS AND THE BEES
Meteor Shower

THE BIRDS AND THE BEES
Squirrel

THE BIRDS AND THE BEES
Swallow Skies

THE BIRDS AND THE BEES
Tree of Life

BUMBLE
Bumble Bee

BUMBLE
Forest Stripe

BUMBLE
Honeycomb

CHIPPER
Chipmunk

CHIPPER
Fox Nap

CHIPPER
Wild Vines

EDEN
Diety

EDEN

Henna

EDEN

Labyrinth

EDEN

Lotus

EDEN
Wildflower

ELIZABETH
Bats in the Belfry

ELIZABETH
16th Century Selfie

ELIZABETH
Ship Shape

FOX FIELD

Foxtrot

FOX FIELD

Baby Geo

FOX FIELD

Hoppy Dot

FOX FIELD

Pony Play

FOX FIELD

Pointed Lace

FLUTTERBY

Bee

FLUTTERBY

Dragonfly Leaves

FLUTTERBY
Butterfly Lace

FLUTTERBY
Snail Paisley

FLUTTERBY
Hexy Tulips

FULL MOON FOREST
Bunny Damask

HUSHABYE
Ducky Dot

HUSHABYE

Owls

MOONSHINE

Swarm

MOONSHINE
Camo Deluxe

MOONSHINE
Lanterns

MOONSHINE

Sprout

NEPTUNE

Making Waves

NEPTUNE
She Sells Sea Shells

NEPTUNE
Triton Turtle

NEPTUNE
The Ravens

NIGHT SHADE
Poison Blossoms

NIGHT SHADE
Scarlet Von Black

NIGHT SHADE

Bella Donna Von Black

NIGHT SHADE

Neptunia Von Black

NEST
Perched

NEST
Bird Town

NEST

Feather Paisley

PRINCE CHARMING
Dandelion

PRINCE CHARMING

Frog Prince

PRINCE CHARMING
Frog

PRINCE CHARMING
Dew Drop

PRINCE CHARMING
Snail Scallop

PLUME
Aviary Dreamscape

PLUME
Feathers

PARISVILLE
Eyedrops

PARISVILLE
Fans

PARISVILLE
French Lace

PARISVILLE
Cameo

PARISVILLE
Sea of Tears

SALT WATER
Tortoise Shell

SALTWATER
Ocean Ponies

SALTWATER
Octo Garden

SALTWATER
Bubble Shells

SALTWATER
Submarines and Seaweed